HimPowered!

Power You Never Knew, For a Life You Could Only Imagine

HimPowered!

Power You Never Knew, For a Life You Could Only Imagine

by

Sherry Ryden

WordCrafts

HimPowered!
Power You Never Knew, For a Life You Could Only Imagine
Copyright © 2014
Sherry Ryden

Unless otherwise noted all Scripture quotations are from the THE HOLY BIBLE, NEW INTERNATIONAL VERSION®, NIV® Copyright © 1973, 1978, 1984, 2011 by Biblica, Inc.™ Used by permission. All rights reserved worldwide.

Scripture quotations marked "NLT" are taken from the *Holy Bible*, New Living Translation, copyright ©1996, 2004, 2007, 2013 by Tyndale House Foundation. Used by permission of Tyndale House Publishers, Inc., Carol Stream, Illinois 60188. All rights reserved.

Scripture quotations marked "NKJV" are taken from Scripture taken from the New King James Version®. Copyright © 1982 by Thomas Nelson. Used by permission. All rights reserved.

Scripture quotations marked "ESV" are from the ESV® Bible (The Holy Bible, English Standard Version®), copyright © 2001 by Crossway, a publishing ministry of Good News Publishers. Used by permission. All rights reserved.

Cover photography by Kenn Stilger
Cover design by David Warren

All rights reserved. No part of this book may be reproduced, stored in a retrieval system, or transmitted in any form or by any means – electronic, mechanical, photocopy, recording, or otherwise – without the prior written permission of the publisher. The only exception is brief quotations for review purposes

Published by WordCrafts Press
Tullahoma, TN 37388
www.wordcrafts.net

Table of Contents

Introduction 1
The Big Reveal 5
The Search Begins 13
How Can I Have the Holy Spirit Living Inside of Me? 18
I'm HimPowered! Now What? 24
The Power of the Holy Spirit In Our Lives 35
The Power of the Holy Spirit Through Us 43
Other Biblical Examples of the Holy Spirit 55
My Current Assignment 66
About the Author 70

Introduction

Amazing success! Wasted years.

Starting anew. Collapse.

A roller coaster life of success-failure-success-failure.

Fearful. Hopeful. Numb.

Yet somehow remaining expectant. Life *has* to be better than this, right?

These words would best describe my life until that fateful day I discovered what should never have been a secret in the first place. Then, simply and only by the grace of God, on a day when there were only two options left: a standoff with God or giving up, did this great, unknown truth become a reality.

So did the standoff, by the way.

It was on that day that I cried out to a God that I had known my whole life; to the Jesus that I had relied on so often as a young girl who spent most of her childhood hiding or living in fear. On that day, I was finally introduced to the most amazing truth that my church had never revealed to me. I no longer had to live this way! I had all the power I could ever need to live the exact life God had created me for.

I learned the truth that at the very moment I had become a follower of Jesus, I also obtained the power to succeed in every area of my life. I had the power to make wise, God-honoring choices. I had the power to tell Fear to take a hike, and it had to obey. ***I had the Holy Spirit living right inside of me***. And I never even knew it.

I did the math and what I realized took me to my knees.

At the time of this Holy Spirit revelation, I was 40 years of age. I had become a follower of Christ at the age of 12. While I feel like I had known Him my whole life, I actually made my public confession of my love for him at that age. That makes at least 28 years where I could have, and should have, lived a much different life. If I had only known, I believe I would have made much better choices. I know I would have slept better.

How many lives could I have impacted for Jesus had I known I had the power to do so? I weep at the thought.

It is because of the Holy Spirit that my life could, and did, change forever.

Such *peace*! Such relief that I didn't have to make every difficult decision on my own. Gone are the days of aimless wandering and wondering. In one moment I said farewell to feeling powerless and helpless and hopeless and fearful. In one moment, in the reading of one scripture, my life was forever changed into one of power and unstoppable purpose. A life I saw other Christians living, yet somehow elusive to me, was now mine.

So many negative adjectives should never befall a true Christian. Such a travesty. Yet so many Christians, true believers and followers of Christ, live a life of existence that only seeks to get into heaven and stay out of hell. We exist, awaiting the rapture. Yet we never truly live, enjoying the power that only comes from Him.

Power to share Jesus.

Power for success.

Power for healing.

Power to tell the devil to get his filthy claws off of us and those we love. So much power!

This book is for every single person that is simply existing, or spiraling in a cycle of success and failure, or living a life of fear or hopelessness. You may be an unbeliever of Jesus. Or like me, a Christian that has never known that incredible gift of the Holy Spirit who comes to reside in you the moment you accept Him as yours.

How sad to go so long not knowing the truth. But that stops. Today.

This book is also a great tool to be used by anyone that ever leads another person to Christ. Please, please, please don't let them spend one day as a new creation in Christ without knowing the gift of the Holy Spirit He so freely gives to them. They need to know they have all the power they could ever need as His follower. If you are in His service, you know firsthand just how important that is. You can't do what you do for Him without the power of the Holy Spirit. Neither can they. But they don't know this yet. You have the awesome privilege of not only leading them to their Savior, you are blessed to be the bearer of even more good news!

Are you ready to be empowered by Him? Or as I now say: HimPowered!

"Are you ready to live *your* HimPowered life?"

Chapter One
The Big Reveal

I feel like I have known Jesus my whole life. I don't remember ever having one of those 'aha' moments or Road To Damascus experiences I've often heard of, where Jesus makes Himself real to people in one amazing moment. For me, He has just always 'been there.' I'm not complaining, believe me. I am so incredibly thankful.

Apparently my family all went to church together when I was a baby, but I don't remember that period of time. My earliest memories do include going to church by myself when I was in elementary school.

I couldn't wait for Sunday to come. My dad would take me and drop me off. My brothers used to tease me by saying I only wanted to see my best friend. They were more right than they knew. Yes, as a young girl living out in the country with only my brothers to see every day, really did look forward to seeing my friend, Kelly. But I was absolutely mesmerized by the Bible stories I learned each week.

Every Sunday, my dad dropped me off just a little down the road from the church. My dime in one hand and my little white Bible in the other, I would literally run into the church and down the stairs to the basement where the youngest Sunday school class was held. It was a tiny little room, with tiny little chairs and a table. My dime would immediately go into the offering envelope and I would excitedly wait for Ms. Bernice to come and teach us.

It was in that small basement classroom where I got to be with my greatest friend, Jesus. He was the one I really came to see each week. I couldn't get enough.

At that time, my home was a very scary place. But on Sunday I went to that little country church and felt so safe. Jesus was there, and somehow, someway, because He was, I just knew nothing bad could happen to me there.

I had no idea Jesus ever left the church, until one night as I was hiding in fear under my bed, He showed up there, too. I couldn't see Him, but I could tell He was right there next to me, keeping me safe. I began talking to Him, in whispers, somehow knowing that He was protecting me, just as I asked.

Jesus has stayed beside me my whole life. Even when I did things that should have pushed Him away, He never left me. I only had to say His name and I instantly felt His presence. Believe me, I caused Him a lot of heartache over my adult life. It breaks my heart to think how I treated Him sometimes. Yet at any time I could just begin talking to Him, and He would be right there, listening to my every word. And protecting me, always protecting me.

It took me 40 years to finally put my relationship with Him as the priority it deserved to be. I will never forget the day that I actually felt my heart change in such a way that I could only describe it as "falling in love." No, not in a romantic sense, but still one where I knew I could never go back to the selfish one-sided relationship it had always been.

I was crazy about Him, and spending time with Him each morning became my favorite part of the day. It was at this time I also discovered that prayer is a two-way street. It's not just me talking to Him, but a conversation between Him and me. He actually does still talk to us, even though we can't see Him in person.

I wrote a little devotion and prayer journal called ***Prayer is a Conversation*** and shared many of my conversations with Him there.

I can only imagine how the original disciples felt, actually being able to touch Him and talk face to face with Him, to feel His love toward them and everyone else He came near. Imagine my shock and disbelief when one day I read the following verse in John 16: *"It is to your advantage that I go away."* (NKJV)

What?! How could anything be better than having Jesus right there with them?

I knew for a fact, and had known since I was a little girl, that *nothing* was better than Jesus! But here He was telling them, and me and anyone who will listen, that because He went away in body, God was able to send the precious third part of the Trinity, the Holy Spirit, to be with all of us. He described how the Spirit would lead me into all truth.

All truth? Wow, what a concept!

I began doing further research in the Bible and discovered that I had received the Holy Spirit at the time of my repentance and acceptance of Christ. I just sat there taking all of this in.

Right here all along, I had God in the form of the Holy Spirit, living inside of me, and I had no clue!

I became more than a little angry that day. I was a bit indignant that in all of my years of going to church, I had never learned this. I'm not blaming anyone, but somehow, someway I missed out on this very important fact.

I began thinking back; way, way back to my earliest memories of church. I remember all of the stories about God and Jesus. But I had no memory of ever learning the truth about the Holy Spirit. Even the name, *Holy Spirit,* was said in a hushed tone, as if saying it out loud would stir up some ghost or something.

I thought about my first time visiting a super charismatic church where people said *Holy Spirit* out loud and often, and they acted like crazy people in there! All that yelling and screaming and running around and jumping. I was terrified! I couldn't wait to escape. I literally ran to my car and locked the door! If that was what *stirring up the Holy Spirit* made people do, I wanted no part of it. No wonder my little country church never mentioned Him!

Oh, but now - now I was being introduced to the real Holy Spirit. The one Jesus talked about. The same Jesus who stayed beside me under the bed many nights as a terrified little girl. The same Jesus who was sitting beside me every morning having coffee 40 years later. My precious best friend was introducing me to the One who lived inside of me because Jesus the man left the earth, and we still had work to do. Now *that* is the Holy Spirit I wanted to learn all about.

Since what very little I knew and believed about the Holy Spirit to that point seemed to be inaccurate, I asked God if He would teach me the truth about Himself in this Spirit form. I began doing Biblical research to discover everything I could about this elusive third part of the Trinity. I refused to listen to any man or woman on TV or read anyone else's opinion. It was just me and God this time. Since God said He would give wisdom freely to all who ask for it (James 1:5) I decided this was a good time to ask for all I could get.

This began the journey that changed my life. I pray that as you read what I am about to share with you in the following chapters of this book, your life will become all that it's meant to be, too.

People often ask me how I came up with this title, ***HimPowered.*** I learned that one of the coolest things the Holy Spirit does for us is He gives us power. I wrote in my prayer journal that day that

I am *empowered* by **Him**. I said it out loud. Then God gave me the word 'HimPowered.' I've been using it and writing about it now for over 10 years.

HimPowered is not a word you will find in the Bible. It's my own word I often use to remind me of how, because of Him, I have all the power I need.

How often do you hear someone say that they feel *empowered* when they hear someone speak or read a good book? I think that word gets overused. Power is not something to take lightly. Perhaps the words *encouraged, motivated* or even *excited* would better fit these examples.

The Bible shares many scriptures about God's power and the power of the Holy Spirit. Nothing can compare to that power. It's truly all any of us could ever need. Being empowered by Him - HimPowered, if you will. It's just my little word, yet I hope that by the time you read the rest of this book, it will be a word that you may want to use to remind you of the Holy Spirit's power within you as a follower of Jesus Christ.

God has been showing me as I teach lifelong church attenders as well as others that are brand new to their faith, that too few people really know who the Holy Spirt is and the incredible power we all have as believers and followers of Christ. If Jesus Himself gave you a promise, wouldn't you think it was important? Especially if it was one of the very last promises He made while still on earth? If you know anything at all about Jesus, you bet you would!

Jesus *promised* the Holy Spirit. God *gave* the Holy Spirit. We can all lead powerful lives, even if you have been in church your whole life but are just now learning the truth about who the Holy Spirit is. Even if you have never heard the name of Jesus and are being introduced to Him right at this very minute. It's not too late.

How do I know?

Here I am, a once frightened, timid, shy little girl that grew into a frequently fearful woman. I once lived a life that appeared so successful at times and a total failure at others. I am now living proof that because of the Holy Spirit, I can live my life, powerful, fearless and effective for Him.

And you can too.

Are you ready?

Chapter 2
The Search Begins

Who IS This Holy Spirit?

Once I began my search for just who the Holy Spirit is, I was totally surprised at all I was reading about Him in the Bible. Since I had made the decision at that time to not look to any other source than the Bible, I knew I could trust the results to be from God Himself, since the Bible is His written words to us. It was so tempting to read the thousands of books written on this subject, but I knew I could trust this one to be all I needed.

So began my journey. As with every journey I take with Him, I had questions. My first question to God went something like this:

Since the Holy Spirit has been someone I should have known more about for so many years, where had all of these scriptures been hiding?

Had I been so blind to these particular passages for so long? Did I just glance over them because I didn't fully understand who He is? I'm sure that's part of it, and yet God revealed even more to me once I honestly sought the answer to this very important question.

I can pick up the exact same Bible every single day and read from it. While it never changes, I certainly do. My life circumstances change. My level of trust can change. My spiritual maturity level changes daily. My questions change.

I can read the exact same scripture today that I read 10 years ago and it will mean so much more depending on where my heart is at the time. For instance, if you have ever attempted to read the Bible, most likely at some point you have read the first few chapters of the very first book, Genesis. All through the very first chapter are the words "God said."

God said, "Let there be light." God said, "Let there be an expanse between the waters." Did you ever wonder who God was talking to? I honestly never did. Then one day while doing this study, I read verse 26: Then God said, "Let **us** make man in **our** image, in **our** likeness…" (emphasis mine)

Whoa, now wait a minute! Just who is this *'us'* and who makes up *'ours'* here? That's plural, right?

And since man had yet to be created, God had to be talking to somebody!

I read it all over again. Do you know what I had totally skipped over every single time I had ever read Genesis? And I mean every single time! Go all the way back to Genesis 1:1: "In the beginning, God created the heavens and the earth. Now the earth was formless and empty, darkness was over the surface of the deep, and the ***Spirit of God*** was hovering over the waters." (emphasis mine)

I had never even noticed that before, and I know I had read it hundreds of times. Right here, in the beginning of the beginning, was the first mention of The Spirit, and I had totally skipped right over it every other time. But because I was finally searching for my answer, and the Bible has every answer to every question we could ever need, I was finally able to see it.

God knows what we can handle. He will reveal everything we need to know right when we need to know it. Seriously, I could spend every day for a solid week just in the first chapter of Genesis and get to a better understanding each and every day. It's true of every other book and chapter of the Bible, too.

Don't beat yourself up if you missed it too, or even if you've never read it. But I encourage you today to pick it up and read it. And do it again tomorrow. Even if it's just Genesis 1:1.

I once read a great quote and I have it written in my Bible: "Don't try to master this book, let the book master me." Let the book master you and your life will never be the same. I promise.

Now, back to this Holy Spirit. I also learned during my search that God was indeed talking to other people in Genesis 1. I believe He was referring to what we call the Holy Trinity - God, Jesus and the Holy Spirit. God in three forms: God, Man and Spirit. While that is a whole topic of study unto itself, let me at least point out that I see Jesus as God in human form and the Holy Spirit as God in spirit form.

Since I already knew who God and Jesus were, and I really loved them, I knew the Holy Spirit wasn't someone I had to be afraid of, like my first church experiences had me believe. And the more I studied and learned about Him, the more I really liked Him, too!

I went back to that chapter that hit me so hard, John 16. Jesus Himself told the disciples to wait for Him (the Holy Spirit) to come and because of this Holy Spirit, they could continue doing so much more than they could ever do on their own.

They were powerless to perform miracles unless Jesus was around, therefore we would be powerless too, all these years later without His physical presence. Since Jesus had to die so that we could have our sins forgiven, then rise again and go to heaven to prepare a place for us, how would the rest of the world come to know Him? Without Jesus here on earth, how would anyone be healed or be convicted of their sins?

Alone, the disciples had no power to perform miracles or lead people to Jesus. And neither do we. That's the work of the Holy Spirit through them, and therefore that is the work of the Holy Spirit through us.

Only God, in the form of the Holy Spirit, has the power to do anything at all of *any* importance to the kingdom. The disciples had Jesus right beside them, but were powerless on their own. They certainly wouldn't have any power without Him, so how else was His work going to continue once He was gone? Since Jesus would no longer physically be on earth, God sent the Holy Spirit, Himself in Spirit form, so that we could always have a part of Him with us. He promised He would never leave us or forsake us. The Holy Spirit is our proof of that promise.

So simple and yet so profound. So God.

Chapter 3
How Can I

Have the Holy Spirit Living Inside of Me?

We know from the previous chapter that the Holy Spirit has been around since the beginning of the beginning. And we can read in other chapters of the Bible that people had been filled with the Holy Spirit even before Jesus was born.

The Old Testament tells us the Holy Spirit spoke through the mouth of David. In the New Testament, Luke 1:67 tells us that Zechariah was filled with the Holy Spirit, and that was certainly prior to Jesus. So what's the difference between this Holy Spirit and the one Jesus told the disciples to wait for?

Since there is only one, it has to be the very same Holy Spirit. The difference is that prior to Jesus leaving earth, the Holy Spirit worked *through* people for an appointed mission, such as to prophesy in the case of Zechariah. He came and went.

But the *gift* of the Holy Spirit that came upon the disciples means that He comes to dwell in *every* believer of Jesus Christ - *and He stays*! Until this time, the Holy Spirit was 'put upon' people, but now He is 'put within' people. Now He is indwelling - living right inside every single one of us that accepts Jesus as their own personal savior.

We read about this first happening in the book of Acts, Chapter 2. It's a great story of how there were 120 people in one room, waiting just as Jesus told them to do. "Suddenly a sound like a blowing of a violent wind came from heaven and filled the whole house where they were sitting. They saw what seemed to be tongues of fire that separated and came to rest on each of them. All of them were filled with the Holy Spirit and began to speak in other tongues as the Spirit enabled them."

Later, Peter addresses the crowds of people that heard this all happening, and reminded them what Joel had prophesied "I will pour out my Spirit on *all* people."

All people. That includes me and that includes you. The gift of the Holy Spirit. A gift from God.

Do you have the Holy Spirit living inside of you? The Bible tells us in Acts 2:38 "Repent and be baptized, every one of you, in the name of Jesus Christ for the forgiveness of your sins. ***And you will receive the gift of the Holy Spirit.*** The promise is for you and your children and for all who are *far off* - for all who the Lord our God will call." (emphasis mine)

I believe these 'far off' could also mean throughout the generations, all the way to you and me today.

If you want this precious gift, then accept Jesus Christ today, right this very minute. In doing so, you will receive not only salvation, but the Holy Spirit as well! Simply say these words: "Jesus, I know that I am a sinner, and I need a savior. I know that you are the son of God and were crucified and died on a cross for my sins. I believe that three days later you came back to life, and are seated at the right hand of the Father. I believe you will return again for me soon and I will live with you in heaven for eternity. Amen"

If you prayed that prayer for the first time, welcome to the family! You are now a child of God, just like Jesus. You can call Jesus your brother. Sweet, huh? And guess what else? You now have the Holy Spirit living right inside of you.

Perhaps you are like me and accepted Jesus many years ago, but had no idea that the Holy Spirit now lives inside of you. Take a moment and think about the awesomeness of that! Let it sink in - God, in spirit form, living right inside of you, right this very moment. Does it take your breath away like it did me? Does it scare you?

Please, there is nothing to be afraid of. God loves you so much He sent Jesus to die for you. And because He didn't want to leave us alone while on this earth, He sent His Spirit to dwell inside our hearts. That's love in the purest form.

But He did not just come to live there. He has a purpose for each of us, and will give us all the power we could ever need, more than we can imagine, to see that purpose fulfilled. You are now empowered by Him. You are now HimPowered!

How cool is that?

You now have salvation, a Biblical term that means you belong to Jesus, and are saved from going to hell. If that alone were not enough, you now also have the presence of the Holy Spirit living inside of you to stay, and the power of the

Holy Spirit to do whatever God has planned for you.

There may be something very specific God has for you, but soon we will talk about a specific assignment we all have as believers of Christ.

A Word of Caution

In 1 John 4, we are warned that not all spirits are the Holy Spirit. How can we tell the real from the imposter? Simple. Put them to the test.

"By this you know the Spirit of God: Every spirit that confesses that Jesus Christ has come in the flesh is of God, and every spirit that does not confess that Jesus Christ has come in the flesh is not of God." (1 John 4:2, 3)

Many false prophets will claim to be from God, and tell you that the Holy Spirit led them to say or do something. Put these prophets to the test as well. A spirit will be behind every prophet, but only a true prophet of God will claim Jesus as the son of God. Since the Holy Spirit will always testify and glorify God, and Jesus as His son, a true prophet will gladly proclaim Jesus as their savior as well, being led by the one and only Holy Spirit to do so.

If someone tries to lead you to receive a spirit, make sure it is truly the Holy Spirit. Later I will share a personal story about a woman that tried to tell me how she helped people find the truth within themselves, claiming it was often from the Holy Spirit, but denied it being from Jesus. Yes, they are out there, and oh so convincing. But now you know the truth.

Chapter 4
I'm HimPowered!

Now What?

If you just accepted Jesus as your savior, I'm so excited for you. You now get to spend eternity with Him in Heaven, in Paradise!

For you veteran Christians, has it sunk in yet that you have the Holy Spirit living inside of you, right now? Pretty cool, huh?

When Jesus left this earth He promised He would go and prepare a place for us. I can't even begin to picture how beautiful Heaven will be. I am thrilled that I will get to see you there. And together we will see Jesus face to face. Incredible!

Think about this: That same Jesus that we have never seen with our own eyes looked 2000 years into the future and saw us. He loved us so much that He allowed Himself to suffer to the point of death so that we have the opportunity to have sin removed from our lives and spend eternity with Him. I am humbled beyond words to even think of being loved so much.

While Heaven will be an awesome place to spend eternity, we still have very important work to do while we are here. Knowing this, God didn't leave us alone.

This is why we have the Holy Spirit.

Can you think of something you would love to be able to do, but within your own ability it's just too difficult, perhaps even impossible? You are not alone. Even the disciples felt this way. They wanted to be able to do the same miracles Jesus did. We are told in John 14 and again in John 16 that the Holy Spirit would be sent to lead and guide us, telling us exactly what we need to know and leading us to do the will of God.

Yes, we still have work to do. And the most important work of all, done only through the power of the Holy Spirit, is to lead others to Jesus, sharing His unfathomable love of them in such a way that they too want to do the will of the Father, and ultimately spend eternity in Heaven with Him and with us.

One of the last statements Jesus spoke right before He ascended up to heaven was recorded in Acts 1:8. "But you will receive power when the Holy Spirit comes on you…" and the rest of His sentence tells us what we should do with that power - "and you will be my witnesses in Jerusalem, and in all Judea and Samaria, and to the ends of the earth."

Since this was the very last thing Jesus spoke, don't you think it's vitally important? Of course it is! What really excites me though, is just how that power can be manifested so that we can actually be His witnesses. Spoken words are often not enough by themselves to convict a person. Some people simply need a demonstration. They must see to believe.

Can you even begin to imagine what having that kind of power running through you could accomplish? The Bible gives us great examples, and one of the first was immediately after the disciples received the Holy Spirit.

If you have ever read the Bible, there is one man that always stands out. Remember Peter? Yes, the very same Peter that denied even knowing Jesus? In case this is a new story for you, I'll fill you in. On his own, Peter (his original name was Simon) was merely a fisherman. He was a simple, uneducated man. One day Jesus came to him and simply said, "Follow me."

Peter followed.

Peter walked with, ate with and witnessed miracles with Jesus. He was one of the original 12 disciples that Jesus chose. He spent every single day with Jesus, promising to defend Him, love Him. Yet when the time came, Peter denied even knowing Jesus. He was still human and still weak and scared because he was still working within his own human abilities.

I know the feeling.

Peter watched Jesus die knowing he had let Him down. Oh, how that must have hurt! But God's purpose for Peter was far from over. It was just beginning. On his own, Peter was just like every one of us - filled with fears and feelings of inadequacy.

And just like Peter, we sin and break God's heart. Every single day.

On his own, Peter was a man that fished for a living, who ran scared and lied about his best friend. On his own, he couldn't share Jesus with even one person. But then something really amazing happened. After Jesus left this earth, He delivered on his promise. He sent the Holy Spirit. Peter, along with many other believers, received the Holy Spirit!

This very same Peter, now filled with the power of the Holy Spirit, could speak to a group of people and watch *3,000* of them repent and be baptized - *in one day*! The same man who was a coward on his own became a brave and powerful apostle for Christ through the Holy Spirit. (Acts 2:14-47)

I would love to have that happen when I speak, yet I am just as thrilled to have one person read this book and come to accept Jesus as their lord and savior because of it.

I am not a professional writer. I am simply a woman chosen by God, filled with the power of the Holy Spirit, writing down every word given to her by the Holy Spirit. I'm telling my story. That's my assignment. If your heart feels different after reading this, that is the Holy Spirit doing *His* job.

Please be very clear on this point, as it's one that tripped me up for quite some time. While it *is* my responsibility (and greatest joy) to share Jesus with others, it is *not* my job to convict them of their sin. Only the Holy Spirit can do that. I make the introduction, He does the rest.

I hope this will take some burden off of you too as you pray for the souls of others and do whatever God gives you the power to do to make this happen.

There was a time in my life when I felt a nudging to share Him, but I didn't know what to do or say on my own. I thought I was going to have to also convince the person to accept Him. I had no idea that God, through the Holy Spirit, would give me the words I needed the moment I opened my mouth. He also does the work in their hearts.

It wasn't up to me!

I was adding more stress than I needed to, worrying about my ability, or lack of ability, to find the right words, or try to bring up the right scripture. Now I know that because of the power of the Holy Spirit, I simply share my story, and His story. Then He reaches into their hearts and makes it possible for them to hear the words as truth.

This is the best news! I don't have to be the next Billy Graham, but I absolutely must be the Holy Spirit-filled Sherry Ryden. And you absolutely must be the Holy Spirit filled _____ (insert your name here)!

Even if you have never memorized one single scripture, the Holy Spirit can empower you to lead another person to Jesus. Even if you just accepted Christ today. Even if you are not educated. Even if you are homeless. Even if you are in prison. Even if you are really old or still very young.

Even if you do not speak one word, your actions and attitude can be used by God to cause a person to wonder, 'Hmmm, something is different about that person, I wonder what it is?'

I discovered a few years ago that a person once accepted Christ because of what I *didn't* do in a relationship. I used very few words, and didn't share a single salvation scripture in this particular case. Yet simply having the Holy Spirit living inside of me caused them to realize that something was missing in their life. Even though our relationship ended, that person went in search of what it could be, and the Holy Spirit showed up to convict their heart.

Frequently I have people come into my home or office, and the tears just start falling. They always say the same thing. "I don't know why I'm crying." I didn't either at first. But one day God revealed to me that His presence was enough to convict their hearts that something was missing in their lives.

I believe that on occasion, some of those people were just as I used to be - Christians who didn't know the Holy Spirit resided inside of them. The Bible tells us that the Spirit Himself testifies with our Spirit that we are God's children. Spirit speaks to Spirit. It was like a 'family reunion' of our hearts as fellow believers of Christ.

He can use you to do the exact same thing. I am so very, very far from perfect. I sin every single day. But I made a choice to be a witness for Jesus, just as He asked before He left earth for heaven. He used the worst sinners mentioned in the Bible, and He uses me. Thank God it's not about me being perfect, just willing. He wants to use you, too.

I don't know about you, but that is a huge relief for me! I don't have to have it all figured out or be a Bible scholar. I just have to be obedient to the prompting of the Holy Spirit, listening for His voice, and follow His instructions for that moment in time. People want to see proof, as they are lied to every single day by those they should be able to trust. Let them see Jesus in you. Then they may listen to you or perhaps years later, to someone else lead them to Christ.

What Not To Do

Now that you know the truth, and hopefully have accepted Christ and have the Holy Spirit living inside of you, other areas of your life may need to change as well.

In every decision or action, consider the very important fact that *You Are Not Alone* in your actions or thoughts. Wherever you go, or even where your mind goes, you take the Holy Spirit, and in essence God, right along with you. How will your life change now? How will your actions, out of your love and loyalty to Christ, be different than before?

There is a story in the Bible about a married couple, Ananias and Sapphira. At this point in early Christian church history, all of the believers were of 'one heart and one soul.' They often sold everything they had and shared everything with each other. They didn't have to, but out of love, they chose to.

This couple also sold some possession, but instead of just keeping some of the proceeds for themselves, they lied about the amount, saying they gave all of the profits. The Bible says they "lied to the Holy Spirit," which is a very interesting verse. Peter told them they had not lied to men, but to God. But what is also very important is the part of the verse where Peter asks "Why has Satan filled your heart to lie to the

Holy Spirit?" It cost them both their lives that day.

That may sound like swift punishment, as we often think of lying as a 'lesser sin.' Yet in this case, all of the believers that gathered together were doing everything out of love for God, and I believe, as a demonstration of God's amazing love for us. There was no selfishness or pride. They did it all out of love. They were siding with God.

When Peter gave Sapphira the chance to tell the truth, she also lied. Peter's response to her gives us so much more insight into what was really going on in her heart: "How is it that you have agreed together to test the Spirit of the Lord?"

The word 'test' in this passage is actually *'peirazo'* the same word used for 'tempt.' It's the same word found in Revelations 2:10, where Jesus says Satan will try to test many of us, his last ditch effort to get us to turn away from God.

Ananias and Sapphira made a deliberate choice to side with Satan. They were not just being selfish, and they were not just lying. They were making a choice to follow Satan instead of God. Satan can still creep into our thoughts and hearts if we allow him to. That is why it is so vitally important to never allow him near us, staying full of the Holy Spirit and taking every thought captive.

We have the power of the Holy Spirt to stop him at the very moment he tries to enter in. We are warned in Revelation 2:10 that this will continue to happen all the way to the end. Yet Jesus also promises us that He will give us the crown of life when we remain faithful.

Chapter 5
The Power of the Holy Spirit

In Our Lives

We have just covered what I believe to be *the* most important role the Holy Spirit plays in our lives - leading others to Jesus. Yet the Bible is full of so many other examples and titles that the Spirit is known for. Let's look first at some of the additional ways the Spirit empowers our lives.

One such title we hear the Spirit called is *'Counselor.'* A counselor is any person who helps someone who is in trouble (with the law). They *testify* on that person's behalf. This is someone, such as an attorney, who helps prove your innocence before a judge.

In John 14:15 Jesus refers to the promised Holy Spirit as 'another' Counselor, a role that the Spirit will undertake as He, like Jesus, will testify to God on our behalf. They will convince God that we have accepted Jesus as His son and our redeemer, therefore allowing us to be found innocent by God on the Day of Judgment. I'd say that's a pretty important Counselor in my life!

On my own, as God is fully aware, I am far from innocent of sin in my life. I do not deserve Heaven; I deserve Hell. Yet through the sacrifice of Jesus, and now through the daily conviction in my life from the Holy Spirit, I will be found blameless before God.

Wow! That humbles me to my knees.

In John 16:7-16 Jesus tells us the Holy Spirit will convict us when we sin. You know that feeling that comes over you right before you start to do something you know is wrong? Or maybe right after you did something you knew you shouldn't do? All along we just called it our conscience. This verse tells us that is the Holy Spirit, giving us the opportunity to make the right decision *not* to sin.

1 Corinthians 10:13 tells us "No temptation has overtaken you except what is common to mankind. And God is faithful; He will not let you be tempted beyond what you can bear. But when you are tempted, He will also provide a way out so that you can endure it."

That *way out* starts with the conviction within your heart by the Holy Spirit. Tune into that *still small voice* and resist the temptation to sin. My life certainly goes much better when I do. And yours will too, I promise.

Before Jesus was born, He was also known as *Counselor*. In Isaiah 9:6, Isaiah calls the promised Messiah the "Wonderful Counselor," indicating the kind of character the coming Christ would have. The word "wonderful" in this passage literally means "incomprehensible." The Messiah will cause us to be "full of wonder." The word has a much stronger meaning than the way it's used in normal conversation today. We tend to say things are "wonderful" if they are the least bit likable. But Jesus is wonderful in a way that is boggling to the mind.

That's the way the Holy Spirit is to me, too. The fact that I have God, in spirit form, living inside of me, simply boggles my mind. The fact that I can be used by Him in any way that is even remotely powerful is more than I can even begin to imagine. Wonderful. Yes! That's my Jesus. And yes, that's the Holy Spirit I want to be full of, don't you?

The Bible tells us that the Holy Spirit is the *Spirit of Truth*. In John 14:6, Jesus tells us that He is the

Way, the Truth and the Life. The way I see it, Jesus is truth in Human form, the Holy Spirit is truth in Spirit form.

When Jesus was on earth, He was the perfect example of all truth to His followers. Whatever He said was absolute truth. Since He ascended back into heaven and gave us the Holy Spirit, we still need someone to show us truth from lies. The Holy Spirit will do just that.

How often in a day's time are we tempted to do something, but not sure if it's really a sin or not? The Holy Spirit will let you know the truth. How often do we think, 'Ah, it won't hurt anyone. It's just me and no one else even has to know.' Well, the Holy Spirit living inside of us knows, and whenever we choose to act on them, we are bringing Him right along with us.

So what kinds of things would that look like? Galatians 5:16-24 spells it out for us:

"But I say, walk by the Spirit, and you will not gratify the desires of the flesh. For the desires of the flesh are against the Spirit, and the desires of the Spirit are against the flesh, for these are opposed to each other, ***to keep you from doing the things you want to do.*** But if you are led by the Spirit, you are not under the law. Now the works of the flesh are evident: sexual immorality, impurity, sensuality, idolatry, sorcery, enmity, strife, jealousy, fits of anger, rivalries, dissensions, divisions, envy, drunkenness, orgies, and things like these. I warn you, as I warned you before, that those who do such things will not inherit the kingdom of God. But the fruit of the Spirit is love, joy, peace, patience, kindness, goodness, faithfulness, gentleness, self-control; against such things there is no law. And those who belong to Christ Jesus have crucified the flesh with its passions and desires." (ESV) (emphasis mine)

So, if I am envious of my friend's new car (or house, or jewelry or whatever), is that Ok? The above scripture says it isn't, and that nagging feeling inside of me is the Holy Spirit telling me to stop thinking such thoughts. Instead I should have joy that my friend is so blessed. That would be evidence of the Holy Spirit controlling my thoughts.

Try it the next time jealousy or any of the above listed sins, or any sin for that matter, tries to overcome you. I promise you will have every opportunity to choose who is in charge of your thoughts or actions: sin from Satan, or righteousness from the Holy Spirit.

Do you belong to Jesus?

If you accepted Him as your Savior you do. Does that mean you will never be tempted to do those things again? Nope, Satan even tried to tempt Jesus, so we are in good company there! What this verse is saying is that when you are filled with the Holy Spirit, you have His power within you to say *No* immediately to the urge to do them.

"Resist the Devil and he will flee." (James 4:7)

You have this power if you are a Christ-follower. When I feel the temptation to sin come over me, I literally say, out loud, 'Satan, you have no authority over me to want to do_____

I command you now, in the name of Jesus and by the power of the Holy Spirit, hit the road! Go back to hell where you belong. You have no power over me.' He *has* to leave you alone if you are a child of God. *Has to*. Not 'maybe'. *Has to!*

The Holy Spirit also empowered Jesus. Isn't that an amazing thought? When I was doing my study of the Holy Spirit's power in my life, this verse from Isaiah 11:1-3 literally made me stop what I was doing to simply take in the magnitude of it.

(1) A shoot will come up from the stump of Jesse; from his roots a Branch will bear fruit.

(2) *The Spirit of the Lord will rest on Him* - the Spirit of wisdom and of understanding, the Spirit of

counsel and of power, the Spirit of knowledge and of the fear of the Lord -

(3) and He will delight in the fear of the Lord.

Do you mean to tell me that the very same Holy Spirit that empowers me also empowered Jesus?

Yes, that's what this scripture says! How amazing is that? Jesus, the son of God, on earth in human form, still needed the Spirit of God to do His work on earth - just like us. Wow.

The 'shoot' mentioned in verse 1 was David. The Branch is Jesus. The Spirit of the Lord is the Holy Spirit, and from the rest of the verse we see His other responsibilities in the life of Jesus. The Holy Spirit gave *all wisdom and understanding, counsel and power, knowledge and fear of the Lord* to Jesus.

He will give you and me whatever measure we need right at the moment we need it.

Do you need wisdom in making a decision? Ask the Holy Spirit.

Do you have trouble understanding a scripture when you are reading your Bible? Ever wonder about a decision God made on your behalf? Ask the Holy Spirt.

Do you seek wise counsel? Do you need power to

share Jesus or complete your God directed assignments? Ask the Holy Spirit.

Do you want to have a better understanding to grasp the awesomeness of God? Yes, the Holy Spirit has been given charge of that in our lives too.

I have often been asked just how I am so absolutely sure there is a God, and that Jesus really did come and die for me. The easy answer is 'faith.' The more realistic answer is that I have faith and believe without a shadow of a doubt because of the Holy Spirit, living inside of me, has revealed this truth to me. He has given me a knowledge and 'fear,' or respect, of the Lord.

I don't need any more proof than that. I don't require signs and wonders and visual miracles. Yet God knew that so many would only be able to truly believe if they had visual proof. In the next chapter, we will talk about many of the ways the Holy Spirit reveals His truth through miracles that never cease to amaze me.

Chapter 6
The Power of the Holy Spirit

Through Us

In the last chapter we looked at all the ways the Holy Spirt works to help *within* us. In this chapter we will cover how the power of the Holy Spirit will work *through* us.

We learned earlier in this book how the disciples of Jesus were powerless on their own. It wasn't until the Holy Spirit filled them that they began to do the same miracles Jesus did. Awesome miracles. The kind of miracles that would take more power than any mere human could possibly have on their own. Supernatural power.

Here is a question that came to my mind and perhaps it did for you too: Can I have that same degree of power?

I know I have the Holy Spirit to counsel and comfort me, and to give me wisdom and discernment when I need to share my faith. That alone is truly enough for me. But what about all of those miraculous acts of healing, driving out demons and other amazing acts of the power of the Holy Spirit? Can I be used by God to do those things as well? In essence, can I have *that* much power?

Of course, just as with every other important question in life, God has His answer waiting for us in His Word.

John 3:34 tells us that "For he whom God has sent utters the words of God, for **He gives the Spirit without measure.**" (NKJV) (emphasis mine) Another translation says He gives the Spirit without *limit*.

Hmm. Some may say that this verse means that only Jesus was given limitless power, but what if it means that those of us filled with the Holy Spirit have all the Spirit's power we could ever begin to need? Limitless power! I'm liking that idea. How about you?

I get more aggravated every day with how Satan keeps taking more and more control over the people I love. He is taking over my country and its leaders. He is leading nations. You may call it Islam or ISIS or by any other name you want. I call him Satan. And I want him stopped.

Satan tries his best to attack our faith. He attacks us in our weakest moments, so it is up to us to stay strong in our faith, spending as much time on our knees in prayer, in fellowship with others and in praising God every chance we get. We are told that God 'inhabits the praise of His people.' I picture Him sitting right next to me when I'm praising Him. How close do you think Satan wants to get to you when God is in the room? I pray for an army of angels to surround and protect me and those I love. I picture them like a sentry, with swords drawn, forming a circle around us.

Yet I know Satan will keep on trying as long as I remain a threat to him. And I fully intend to remain a threat to him, as I fully intend to share the love of Christ and the power of the Holy Spirit with anyone that will listen when I'm prompted by Him to speak. Satan cannot touch me without God's permission, so I have nothing to fear. Neither do you if you are a child of God.

He promises us in Romans 8:15: "For you did not receive a spirit that make you a slave again to fear." Because of the power of the Holy Spirit within us as heirs in God's kingdom, we can be as fearless as Jesus in doing God's will in our lives.

Are you ready to finally be forever free of the spirit of fear that creeps in every time you take a step forward? Tap into the power of the Holy Spirit that lives inside of you. Just like any other ugly spirit from Satan, the spirit of fear must also flee when you tell him to.

Tell him to flee, now! Tell him again when he tries again, because he will keep trying if he thinks he can get away with it.

Fellow believers, what if we really tapped in to the *limitless* power we have within us? What could that look like in the lives of those we love? Could God, through the power of the Holy Spirit, use us to heal? I believe so. I'm living proof.

Many years ago I became deathly ill. What started as flu-like symptoms began to weaken me to the point of becoming almost paralyzed on one side. My doctor ran every test but nothing came back. An MRI showed 'something on my hypothalamus' but they were not sure what it was.

I was given three possibilities: a brain tumor, a stroke or a virus. He said he hoped it was a tumor because I would be dead within days if it was anything else. We were told to call in the family.

I was too weak and sick at that point to even sit up in bed. I hadn't eaten in almost a month. I had lost over 20 pounds, couldn't walk or even comb my own hair.

The brain surgeon, literally seconds before they were ready to shave my head, stopped all proceedings, saying it was so deep that I would be a vegetable if they drilled that far in. I was placed in ICU with one-on-one monitoring so that 'when' I stopped breathing, they would put me on a ventilator, because they didn't know what else to do with me.

We were new to the area, and the pastor of the church we had just begun attending came to visit me. He asked me if I had ever been anointed with oil. I hadn't and didn't really understand what that meant. He then asked me the most important question he could: "Do you believe that Jesus can heal you?"

Ah, now *that* I understood! I knew Jesus from way, way back. My best friend, Jesus? That same Jesus that stayed with me while I was hiding under the bed? The same Jesus that never left my side my whole life? Yes, I knew *that* Jesus, and somehow I *believed* that Jesus would heal me. He had never let me down yet.

I said 'Yes, Jesus can heal me.'

And Jesus did.

I was home three days later.

That sweet pastor and his wife were used by God to save my life that day. They tapped into the power of the Holy Spirit to anoint me and pray for my healing. I was just like the woman we read about in Matthew 9:22: Jesus turned and saw her. *"Take heart, daughter,"* he said, *"your faith has healed you."* And the woman was healed at that moment. And so was I.

I am a daughter of the King. My King, my God, through the power of the Holy Spirit, took my simple faith and healed me that day. In that moment my life was spared, and in that moment, my life was changed forever.

Can Jesus heal you? Yes, He can. Did that pastor heal me? No. But he used the power of the Holy Spirit in his life to touch me with the healing power of Jesus.

There have been other times I've been instantly healed when someone has prayed for me. It's saved me from surgery more than once. I know others that have as well. I have prayed for others to be healed and they have received immediate healing. It wasn't me. It was the power of the

Holy Spirit through me, and their faith that healed them.

Do you know what a conduit is? The dictionary tells us that it's 'something or someone that is used as a way of sending something from one place or person to another.' There are electrical or water or other types of conduits. They allow energy, for instance, to move from its power source to where that power is needed. That's how I see us being used by God to transmit His power source, the Holy Spirit, to another person. That pastor was a conduit to me. The healing power of the Holy Spirit in his life, transferred over to me, and though faith, I was healed.

My first career was in the medical field. I have witnessed many people go from life to death and back to life again. I have been a part of hundreds of "Code Blue" teams. I believe God uses medical miracles all the time.

I remember one time I was working in a small free-standing unit where most patients who were too sick to go home but not critical enough to stay in the hospital came to live. Most came there to live out the rest of their days. One particular day I responded to a Code Blue in a patient's room. We gave her CPR, but nothing worked. She could not breathe on her own, and her heart had stopped beating. They stopped the Code and pronounced her dead.

Something inside of me said, "Not yet, it's not her time yet." I prayed for her, told the team what I believed and asked them to wait. I gave her a couple more breaths. Within seconds this precious elderly woman started breathing again! The whole room was astonished. She was alive. She eventually went home to be with her family. I believe two miracles happened that day.

While I have not been a part of seeing a person that has been dead for a few days come back to life, I've heard stories from other Christians that have witnessed it, especially in other countries. Sadly, in America, our faith had been so watered down that I think we stifle the work of the Holy Spirit in and through us. I have decided to be bold in my faith, and have begun to expect miracles when I pray. And the more I believe, the more I get to witness those miracles.

Another way we can be a conduit of the Holy Spirit is to drive out demonic forces or evil spirits from our lives and the lives of others. This is a tricky area to talk about and one that many people don't want anything to do with. I know it was scary to me at first, yet I've come to believe that while this is not something that should be played around with, it's also not anything we need to fear.

As we already discussed, Fear itself is a spirit, as we are told in 2 Timothy 1:7 "For God has not given us a spirit of fear, but of power and of love and of a sound mind." (NKJV)

I think that Hollywood has gone a long way to cause us to be fearful when we, as believers of Christ, simply do not have to put up with the devil and his followers. They produce movies about demons and zombies and walking dead people. It's enough to cause nightmares in just about anybody. Yet no one bothers to show the other side - the side where Holy Spirit-filled followers of Jesus Christ, simply through faith and the power of the name of Jesus, can send them all packing!

A word of caution here: If you have not accepted Christ and do not have the power of the Holy Spirit, may I warn you to not mess with this. The Bible gives us an example of what happens to those that try to throw around the name of Jesus, but do not have a relationship with Him and therefore no authority to do so.

Acts 19: 13-17 reveals this example to us: "Some Jews who went around driving out evil spirits tried to invoke the name of the Lord Jesus over those who were demon-possessed. They would say, "In the name of Jesus whom Paul preaches, I command you to come out." Seven sons of Sceva, a Jewish chief priest were doing this. One day the evil spirit answered them. "Jesus I know, and Paul I know, but who are you?" Then the man who had the evil spirit jumped on them and overpowered them all. He gave them such a beating they ran out of the house naked and bleeding. When this became known to the Jews and Greeks living in Ephesus, they were all seized with fear and the name of Jesus was held in high honor."

Now *that* is a movie I'd pay to see!

I love that last verse where we are reminded to hold the name of Jesus in high honor. His is not a name to be thrown around lightly. His name is power and should be used only when we are in right standing with Him.

The same holds true for the Holy Spirit. I recently had an interesting conversation with a woman that told me she helps people find all the answers they need 'within themselves.' She went on to say that it's often a 'spiritual experience.' She then took it a step further with comments that made me shudder. She stated that often 'the spirit' was the Holy Spirit. When I asked her if she meant the same Holy Spirit that we receive as Christians when we accept Jesus, she literally smirked at me and shook her head.

I looked her straight in the eye and said 'We cannot have the Holy Spirit without Jesus.' Again, she just gave me that look and shook her head. I repeated my statement. After rolling her eyes at me, she said we just needed to move on to another topic. The truth made her very uncomfortable.

I couldn't believe what I was hearing! Here is a woman charging money to 'help people' and feeding them a lie so big it makes my heart hurt. Most of the time I meet people like myself that have accepted Jesus but don't understand that we have the Holy Spirit. Here was a woman that actually believes she has the Holy Spirit without Jesus! I pray that she learns the truth before it's too late.

Now, let's get to the best part!

Yes, it's so wonderful to have the power of the Holy Spirit to heal people and rebuke the demons that try to ruin our lives, but let's not forget what is *most* important here. The story in Luke 10: 17-20 is both an exciting promise and a precious reminder:

"The seventy-two returned with joy, saying, "Lord, even the demons are subject to us in your name!" And he said to them, "I saw Satan fall like lightning from heaven. Behold, I have given you authority to tread on serpents and scorpions, and over all the power of the enemy, and nothing shall hurt you. Nevertheless, do not rejoice in this, that the spirits are subject to you, ***but rejoice that your names are written in heaven.***" (emphasis mine)

Yes! Now *that* is a truth worth celebrating! Because of Jesus, we are empowered to do everything He sends us to do. Yet most importantly, our names are written in heaven, where we will get to spend an eternity with Him.

Chapter 7
Other Biblical Examples
of the Holy Spirit

Anointing Oil of Prophets, Priests and Kings

In the last chapter we talked about the Holy Spirit being represented by oil, often used for healing. In the Old Testament, oil was often poured on the heads of the prophets, priests and kings, representing the flow of anointing from leadership down to the people. Today, we represent those same roles as we share Christ with others and make important decisions for those in our care.

As prophets, we are called to speak to others as the Holy Spirit leads us. There have been many times I have been praying for someone and the Holy Spirit prompted me to share just the right word or scripture with them, just what they needed to hear at that moment. I'm not a mind reader, so how else would I have known what they were going through, or perhaps had been praying about? Acts 2:17 tells us "Your sons and daughters will prophesy." We can come to expect to be used like this often when we allow the Holy Spirit to speak through us.

Like the priests of old, we are called to worship and lead others to worship as well. Some may be called in a greater leadership role of a church, and will need every ounce of Holy Spirit power to prepare, teach, lead and pastor their flock. However, as His followers, Jesus gave *all* of us the responsibility to lead others to God.

Remember, His very last words, spoken immediately before He was taken back up to heaven, gave us the main reason for receiving the power of the Holy Spirit - in order to be His witness throughout the world. We are *all* priests in that manner, and it's not just for the 'paid professional' leading the local church. However, for some specifically, as in Isaiah, 61:1, the Lord may anoint us to 'preach good news to the poor.'

As kings (yes this applies to women, too), we can take whatever leadership roles God has placed us in, and through the power of the Holy Spirit be anointed to make decisions and take authority to lead and protect our businesses and households.

Wouldn't it be wonderful if all professional leaders would call on the Holy Spirit to lead them to make the best decisions for our country, states, towns and communities? Would you prefer to work for a boss that simply calls all the shots, or one who seeks God's direction for the business that provides an income for you and your family?

As a leader, chosen by God, ask daily for a fresh anointing to fulfill your responsibilities. You do not have to face each day alone, although it may often seem like it. The Holy Spirit will pour out everything you need to refresh and sustain you, granting you wisdom and power to fulfill your duties.

This goes for husbands as the leaders of your homes, and to the single women and mothers that do not currently have a husband to lead them. That makes you the leader, and I know firsthand how desperately I needed the power of the Holy Spirit to make decisions for myself and my son for so many years as a single mother. I also needed His refreshing, comforting presence each and every day.

A Very Special Oil

Further in Isaiah, we learn about the 'oil of joy' or 'oil of gladness' instead of mourning. Perhaps the Holy Spirit will be poured out on you to comfort those who grieve. What a beautiful, precious assignment.

A Dove

One of the most beautiful examples of the Holy Spirit, and certainly my favorite visual example, is how He appeared the moment Jesus was baptized. Mark 1:10 tells us "As Jesus was coming up out of the water, he saw heaven being torn open and the Spirit descending on him like a dove."

A dove. What can be more gentle and peaceful than a dove? That's the Holy Spirit. Pure, yet powerful. Gentle, yet gets His job done when we cooperate, as Jesus did in the very next verse: "At once the Spirit sent him out into the desert, and he was in the desert forty days, being tempted by Satan."

Once we become more in tune with the Holy Spirit's leading in our lives, He may also come upon us, like a dove, gently leading us to wherever God wants us to go. Yet, where we initially end up may be a very difficult place. Like Jesus, it may be a time of fasting. It may be a time of testing. It may indeed be a very dark place, as is often the case when the enemy comes in to try to interfere with God's plan for our lives.

I think we can also learn from this verse that once our anointing occurs, Satan will be the first one there to try to stop us. We may not immediately recognize him as Satan, yet the Spirit will reveal all truth to us. This is a very important lesson to remember: since the Spirit only does what God tells Him to do, (John 16:13) and God allowed His own Son to be tempted, God will also allow the same to happen to us.

At the time it's happening, it may feel like abandonment or punishment, yet God is preparing us for an even greater assignment and this time of testing and tempting, hunger and thirst, may be a precious, historical period of our lives. It is at this critical moment we are to remember that God is all we need. It's also a crucial time to remember what we learned previously: He will also always give us a way out.

Now that we have the power of the Holy Spirit, we also have the power to say 'Away from me, Satan!' just as Jesus did. Gotta love it!

Wind & Fire

When the Holy Spirit came upon the disciples and others at Pentecost, He arrived 'suddenly, like a sound of the blowing of a violent wind and filled the whole house.' He then appeared like 'tongues of fire that separated and came to rest on each of them.'

Wow, that had to be an incredible experience! I've read it once described as wind like a hurricane or tornado, loud and violent. It had to be loud, as people in the city heard it and came running to see what had made the noise. Wind can be forceful and when it hits it can clear everything in its path. It can pick up a whole house and place it in another location.

Perhaps that is what needed to happen to the disciples at that moment. They were all sitting in a room, awaiting their next assignment, just as Jesus instructed. Yet the Holy Spirit was about to come upon them and move them to 'the ends of the earth,' also just as Jesus commanded.

Fire was often used to purify gold and other metals, as was discussed in Numbers 31. One day we will all need to be found pure, holy and blameless, and the Holy Spirit will convict us when we are not. We can then seek forgiveness and be cleansed of all unrighteousness. That is what Jesus did for us when He shed His blood on the cross. He paid the price, in advance, so that when the Holy Spirit comes upon us revealing every sin we need to seek forgiveness for, we can be found pure and refined as gold.

Wind and fire. Powerful and penetrating, burning into our very souls to change and purify us.

Water

I love the refreshing passage in John 7:37-39: "On the last and greatest day of the Feast, Jesus stood and said in a loud voice, 'If anyone is thirsty let him come to me and drink. Whoever believes in me as the Scripture has said, streams of living water will flow from within him.' By this He meant the Spirit, whom those who believed in Him were later to receive. Up to that time the Spirit had not been given, since Jesus had not yet been glorified."

Do you ever feel dry or empty? Call on the Holy Spirit to fill you with His flowing streams of living water. Nothing can ever be as refreshing as flowing water. Cool, fresh and never ending, flowing in and through us, bringing in the fresh anointing we need, and flushing out anything that is no longer pure or necessary in our lives.

So often, especially for those in ministry, counseling or other leadership roles, there is simply no one else to talk to and unburden all that has been shared with them. This can also be said of single mothers or fathers, those in prison, those without a loving home church or group of fellow believers, and especially those in the mission fields so far away from home. Ask God to fill and refresh you. He promises He will.

Jesus specifically was speaking of those that are truly empty of Him and the Holy Spirit. Jesus is literally, through the Holy Spirit, speaking to those who believe they have nowhere to turn. Is this you? Turn to Jesus, just as He said, and drink in His goodness and mercy. He will fill you with His Holy Spirit the very instant you do.

There is no time like the present. What are you waiting for?

Once you receive Jesus and therefore are immediately filled with the Holy Spirit, that same fresh water can pour out from you to others. The world is parched, dry and empty. What a blessing to be able to share this Living Water with everyone, assuring them that they too can be filled and in turn, pour out to others that need Jesus and the power of the Holy Spirit in their lives.

Picture a fountain, filled with fresh, pure water. It rises upward, then flows down and out, filling every dry area, ultimately being drawn back to the top to be refreshed and poured back out again. Are you seeking your ultimate purpose in life? I cannot think of a greater purpose than this, can you?

Supernatural Conception

I've purposefully left this one for last. While it has to be one of the most precious acts of the Holy Spirit, it is not one we can emulate or take on for ourselves. Yet it still causes awe and wonder to imagine. Take a moment to sit back and take all of this in.

At the time of this writing, it's the Christmas season. With it brings the beautiful story of Mary, her miraculous conception and ultimately the birth of Jesus. In reading it for about the 1000th time, I'm once again reminded of the matchless power of the Holy Spirit to do what only God can do.

Only God could put Himself in human form. Only God, through the Holy Spirit, could cause a virgin to conceive and deliver a baby. The Messiah, no less! And while it's not written in this passage, I have to imagine that this same Holy Spirit brought comfort and assurance to cause Mary to take her from bewilderment to sing a song of praise, written so beautifully in Luke 1:46-55. I hope you will read it again, this time from a little different perspective.

Earlier in this chapter of Luke, we are witness to Elizabeth being filled with the Holy Spirit at the mere sound of Mary's voice. Elizabeth was pregnant with the same John who would ultimately baptize Jesus. This is the only account I can find of a person being filled with the Holy Spirit before he was even born, but this is exactly what the angel had said would happen in Luke 1:15: "He will also be filled with the Holy Spirit, even from his mother's womb." (NKJV)

In Conclusion

God has a plan for our lives before we are even born. I believe He often creates the plan, then creates the person to fulfill it. We will need the power of the Holy Spirit to fulfill that assignment. John the Baptist received his power before birth as God had a remarkable plan for him that only one man could fulfill.

Before Jesus, the Holy Spirit filled those that God chose at the moment of His choosing. Yet you and I have the awesome honor of receiving the power of the Holy Spirit at the very moment we accept Jesus as our Lord and Savior. The minute we belong to Him, our greatest purpose can begin. For at that moment we receive salvation, we also receive the promised Holy Spirit. With that power, we can share Christ with others so that they too may know this amazing gift and fulfill their own purpose in this world.

My Current Assignment

A few years ago I was seeking God for the next direction in my life; my next assignment. I sensed Him telling me to, 'Write the book.'

I had no idea what that meant. I wasn't a writer. I asked Him what book I was supposed to write. I then went to my Bible to see what He might say.

At that very moment, God took me to a tiny little book in the Bible called Habakkuk. I read the second chapter and it caused a whole new sensation to stir within me. "Write down the revelation and make it plain on tablets so that a herald may run with it. For the revelation awaits for an appointed time."

Now, I know that was God speaking to Habakkuk way back then. But could these words also be meant for me now? Just in case, I started writing everything God started saying to me. It was at this time that the word ***HimPowered*** first came to me. The appointed time had come, as God revealed the truth of His Holy Spirit to me.

I've been writing about being *HimPowered* for many years now in my own journal. I have been acting on this power whenever the Spirit leads me to. It's so exciting to see lives changed! Then, just a few days ago, I began feeling a stirring within, from the Holy Spirit. If you are familiar with the Holy Spirit, you know what I'm talking about. If not, I can only describe it as a special feeling I get when God is trying to get my attention. I only (and always) feel this way right before something great from God is about to happen. It always causes me to stay extra alert to everything around me and inside of me. Once He comes to dwell inside of you, you will know this feeling for yourself.

I didn't know what this particular stirring was all about, so I waited to see if God revealed anything else. He told me to go again to that little chapter in Habakkuk. I did. I even wrote about it in my prayer journal.

"What now, God?" I asked.

He said, 'Wait.'

So I waited. Until today.

In my quiet time this morning, I once again asked

God what my next assignment was. He told me to read Habakkuk again.

I prayed with my prayer group this morning for God to reveal His next steps for me. I wanted to make sure I was paying attention. Then later I saw a title of an upcoming book release by a famous author and my stomach did a flip flop. It had a title that contained one of the words I had considered using in my subtitle if I ever wrote a book. Memories of God's instructions came flooding in. "Write the book."

Moments later the receptionist at my office told me I had a package. I opened it to find a totally different book sent me by someone I barely knew. I didn't recognize the title, but directly below the title was the verse from Habakkuk 2:2. Coincidence? Not on your life!

I knew God was giving me my next assignment. He was telling me to take the lessons He has been giving me for over 10 years and 'Write the book!' This is *my* appointed time. Time to write the book He has been preparing me to write, using the word *HimPowered* that He gave me as the title.

I originally had a completely different subtitle in mind, but just didn't feel at peace with it. I began praying for God to give me just the right one. He asked me who my target audience would be. I knew it was mainly people just like me that previously had no idea that they already had the Holy Spirit living inside of them, nor of the power they could tap into whenever necessary to live a life they had only dreamed about in the past.

Next would be anyone who is searching for a better life - a life that only Jesus can give.

I went to my white board and immediately wrote these words:

HimPowered! *Power You Never Knew, For A Life You Could Only Imagine*

Perfect.

He has given me every word to write. He has led me to every scripture to share. I pray it has strengthened and encouraged you as much as it did me while writing it. But more than that, I pray God uses this book to reveal to you the amazing power we have as His children and followers of Jesus, so that your life will also be better than you could ever imagine.

Once He does, I will have to ask:

"Are you finally ready to live *your* **HimPowered** *life?*"

About the Author

Sherry Ryden is a woman on a mission. Her greatest desire is to have every single person she meets 'know God a little better and love God even more.'

As the founder of HimPowered Living, she utilizes her 30 plus years in the corporate world to assists others to live God-honoring lives, and to start or run successful, God-honoring businesses.

A sought after speaker and author, Sherry also works as a consultant to businesses, helping them grow to greater success and profitability.

Connect with Sherry online at:

www.sherryryden.com

You might also enjoy these fine books from:

WordCrafts Press

ProVerb Ponderings
    (31 Ruminations on Positive Action)
  by Rodney Boyd

Morning Mist
    (Stories from the Water's Edge)
  by Barbie Loflin

Why I Failed in the Music Business
    (and how NOT to follow in my footsteps)
  by Steve Grossman

Youth Ministry is Easy!
    (and 9 other lies)
  by Aaron Shaver

Chronicles of a Believer
  by Don McCain

Illuminations
  by Paula K. Parker & Tracy Sugg

www.wordcrafts.net

www.ingramcontent.com/pod-product-compliance
Lightning Source LLC
Chambersburg PA
CBHW072105290426
44110CB00014B/1841